The Twe
of Ch

Volume Seven

ex libris

Candlestick Press

Published by:
Candlestick Press,
Diversity House, 72 Nottingham Road, Arnold, Nottingham NG5 6LF
www.candlestickpress.co.uk

Design, typesetting, print and production by Diversity Creative
Marketing Solutions Ltd., www.diversity.agency

Introduction and selection © Carol Ann Duffy, 2015

Cover illustration 'Seven Swans-A-Swimming'
from 'The Twelve Days of Christmas',
© Lizzie Adcock, www.arumliliedesigns.co.uk

© Candlestick Press, 2015

ISBN 978 1 907598 34 0

Acknowledgements:

Our thanks to Carol Ann Duffy for her continuing generosity.

Thanks also to Julian Stannard for permission to print 'Happy Carp Christmas';
to Adam Horovitz for 'Orcop Christmas'; to Lachlan Mackinnon for 'Christmas
Eve'; to Paula Meehan for 'The Ghost Song' and to Carol Ann Duffy for 'The
Lineage'. 'Christmas Pudding' from *Human Work* by Sean Borodale is © Sean
Borodale 2015. Published by Jonathan Cape 2015. Reproduced by permission
of the author c/o Rogers, Coleridge and White Ltd, 20 Powis Mews, London
W11 1JN. Jane Hirschfield, 'A Chair in Snow', from *The Beauty* (Bloodaxe
Books, 2015) is reproduced in the UK by kind permission of Bloodaxe Books.
In the USA, 'A Chair in Snow' from *The Beauty: Poems by Jane Hirschfield* ©
Jane Hirschfield, 2015, is used by permission of Alfred A Knopf, an imprint of
the Knopf Doubleday Publishing Group, a division of Penguin Random House
LLC. All rights reserved. Theo Dorgan, 'A Woman in Winter' from *Nine Bright
Shiners* (Dedalus Press, 2014) is reproduced by kind permission of the author and
Dedalus Press. 'Saint Nicholas' from *The Poems of Marianne Moore* is © Estate
of Marianne Moore and is reprinted by permission of Faber and Faber Ltd. In
the USA, 'Saint Nicholas' is copyright © 1958 by Marianne Moore; copyright
renewed © 1986 by Lawrence E. Brinn and Louise Crane, Executors of the Estate
of Marianne Moore, from *The Poems of Marianne Moore* by Marianne Moore,
edited by Grace Schulman. Used by permission of Viking Books, an imprint of
Penguin Publishing Group, a division of Penguin Random House LLC. Our thanks
to The Random House Group Ltd for permission to reprint Liz Berry, 'Christmas
Eve', from *Black Country* (Chatto & Windus, 2014) and to Pan Macmillan for
permission to reprint Colette Bryce, 'Magi', from *The Whole & Rain-domed
Universe* (Picador, 2014).

While every effort has been made to secure permission to reprint material
protected by copyright, we will be pleased to make good any omissions brought
to our attention in future printings of this pamphlet.

Where poets are no longer living, their dates are given.

Contents

Introduction

It is a great pleasure to invite you to this year's twelve Christmas poems. This is the seventh pamphlet of Christmas poems that I have edited for Candlestick Press, and I suspect that my own Christmas would feel quite strange without the process of choosing the year's poems. I hope that you, too, enjoy these annual Christmas offerings, and that reading the poems each year has come to represent a bubble of peace at such a busy time. Some of the poems this year have already been published elsewhere; others are new work printed here for the first time.

This year's poems seemed to come together as if they had turned up at the same moment at a party, to share their thoughts, their humanity, their songs, boisterous or quiet, uproarious or mournful. Some of the poems, like Liz Berry's 'Christmas Eve', arrived only to take off their coat and stare out of the window (at a world "tinselled by sleet" where tower blocks "are advent calendars/ every curtain pulled to reveal a snow-blurred face"). Other poems suggested a sense of lineage, like Theo Dorgan's "tree her mother planted years ago" for the benefit of future generations. My own poem, likewise, is concerned with unbroken, invisible lines. A different tree, this time a hawthorn that died in a storm in Adam Horovitz's 'Orcop Christmas', highlights how easily the landmarks of our lives and narratives can leave an absence in the place where they once stood.

The medieval knight Gawain makes a couple of guest appearances this year, while an anonymous sixteenth-century poem takes us back to the mead hall, the focus of early Christmas festivity. Some poems are panoramic and full of props, others clear out the clutter of life to highlight a single figure or object in a landscape, like Jane Hirschfield's 'A Chair in Snow'.

At the end of a year in which wars and natural disasters have turned so many people into refugees, enduring misery and shaming our governments, Lachlan Mackinnon's poem 'Christmas Eve' suggests a wholly appropriate contemporary twist to the Christmas story. Nor could I resist Julian Stannard's 'Happy Carp Christmas' or Marianne Moore's 'Saint Nicholas', a pure joy from start to finish.

This year, we are supporting the British Red Cross with a donation from sales of the pamphlet.

I hope that you enjoy reading the poems as much as I enjoyed choosing them.

Happy Christmas!

Carol Ann Duffy

A Woman in Winter

She walks the ditch, contented and alone,
sends up a flight of crows with every stone.

Beyond the ridge, beyond the frost-gripped fence
the light pours down on lands of innocence.

A tree stands out against the winter snow,
a tree her mother planted years ago.

The sun flares up, and shines through bitter cold
on sudden flashing ornaments of gold.

Theo Dorgan

Christmas Eve

It was late, and the woman pale with fear,
The husband elderly, the donkey zonked.
I wished them well, but couldn't have them here.
Travelling reps and local girls vin blanc'd
Half senseless were at full pitch in both bars,
Food flying from the kitchen and the rooms
All spoken for – not quite Harper's Bazaar's
Notion of glitz, but not just ee-bah-gooms.

These rather sweet, provincial, pious folk
Wouldn't fit in and might put people off.
Horses for courses. Nods. We hardly spoke.
They left. They're born survivors. Caesar's tough
Taxes have nearly brought me to my knees.
Why should I have to harbour refugees?

Lachlan Mackinnon

Orcop Christmas

That final Christmas, I hunted for Orcop's holy thorn
along lanes narrowed by bronze-black leaves,
peered through hedgerows starved of birdsong
into winter-dithered pasture, sought the miraculous
promissory wink of white December stars.

I found no field-feast of light, no hawthorn
where I'd read it stood, just cigarettes in the verge,
nine rattling in a twenty box. I climbed a tree,
belched gouts of votive smoke across the lane
and, for the last time willingly, I prayed.

Back home, my mother said *A Christmas quest!*
and laughed although it hurt. She held my cheek.
You're not quite Galahad, more Gawain with that hair.
The thorn died in a storm two years ago. I'm sure I said...
Tear-clenched, I withdrew

until fire lit the kitchen for a feast. We sat to eat,
firm rods of lurcher chin pressed to our laps,
witness to the one small miracle the day allowed:
my mother, briefly strong again amongst
the hedgerow hallows that wreathed the room

a passing grace that hid in smoke
the way the cancer kept shaving her to light.

Adam Horovitz

Christmas Eve

Tonight the Black Country is tinselled by sleet
falling on the little towns lit up in the darkness
like constellations – the Pigeon, the Collier –
and upon the shooting stars of boy racers
who comet through the streets in white Novas.
It's blowing in drifts from the pit banks,
over the brown ribbon of the cut, over Beacon Hill,
through the lap-loved chimneys of the factories.
Sleet is tumbling into the lap of the plastercast Mary
by the manger at St Jude's, her face gorgeous and naïve
as the last Bilston carnival queen.
In the low-rise flats opposite the cemetery,
Mrs Showell is turning on her fibre-optic tree
and unfolding her ticket for the rollover lottery
though we ay never 'ad a bit o luck in ower lives
and upstairs in the box-rooms of a thousand semis
hearts are stuttering and minds unravelling
like unfinished knitting.
And the sleet fattens and softens to snow,
blanking the crowded rows of terraces
and their tiny hankies of garden, white now, surrendering
their birdfeeders and sandpits, the shed Mick built
last Autumn when the factory clammed up.
And the work's gone again
and the old boys are up at dawn to clock-on nowhere
except walk their dogs and sigh
at the cars streaming to call centres and supermarkets
because there ay nuthin in it that's mon's werk,
really bab, there ay...

But it's coming down now, really coming
over the stands at the Molineux, over Billy Wright
kicking his dreams into the ring road
and in the dark behind the mechanics
the O'Feeney's boy props his BMX against the lock-ups
and unzips to piss a flower into the snow
well gi' me strength, Lord, to turn the other cheek
fer we'm the only ones half way decent round ere
and the tower blocks are advent calendars,
every curtain pulled to reveal a snow-blurred face.
And it's Christmas soon, abide it or not,
for now the pubs are illuminated pink and gold
The Crooked House, Ma Pardoes, The Struggling Mon
and snow is filling women's hair like blossom
and someone is drunk already and throwing a punch
and someone is jamming a key in a changed lock
shouting *for christ's sake, Myra, yo'll freeze me to jeth*
and a hundred new bikes are being wrapped in sheets
and small pyjamas warmed on fireguards
and children are saying *one more minute, just one, Mom*
and the old girls are watching someone die on a soap
and feeling every snow they've ever seen set in their bones.
It's snowing on us all
and I think of you, Eloise, down there in your terrace,
feeding your baby or touching his hand to the snow
and although we can't ever go back or be what we were
I can tell you, honestly, I'd give up everything I've worked for
or thought I wanted in this life,
to be with you tonight.

Liz Berry

Saint Nicholas,

      might I, if you can find it, be given
a chameleon with tail
that curls like a watch spring; and vertical
on the body – including the face – pale
  tiger-stripes, about seven;
  (the melanin in the skin
  having been shaded from the sun by thin
    bars; the spinal dome
      beaded along the ridge
    as if it were platinum)?

    If you can find no striped chameleon,
might I have a dress or suit –
I guess you have heard of it – of *qiviut*?
and to wear with it, a taslon shirt, the drip-dry fruit
  of research second to none;
    sewn, I hope, by Excello;
    as for buttons to keep down the collar-points, no.
      The shirt could be white –
        and be "worn before six,"
      either in daylight or at night.

But don't give me, if I can't have the dress,
a trip to Greenland, or grim
trip to the moon. The moon should come here. Let him
make the trip down, spread on my dark floor some dim
  marvel, and if a success
    that I stoop to pick up and wear,
      I could ask nothing more. A thing yet more rare,
        though, and different,
          would be this: Hans von Marées'
      St. Hubert, kneeling with head bent,

    erect – in velvet and tense with restraint –
hand hanging down: the horse, free.
Not the original, of course. Give me
a postcard of the scene – huntsman and divinity –
  hunt-mad Hubert startled into a saint
    by a stag with a Figure entwined.
    But why tell you what you must have divined?
Saint Nicholas, O Santa Claus,
        would it not be the most
          prized gift that ever was!

Marianne Moore (1887 – 1972)

Now is the time of Christmas

> Make we mery bothe more and lasse,
> For now is the time of Christimas.

Let no man cum into this hall,
Grome, page nor yet marshall,
But that sum sport he bring withal,
For now is the time of Christmas.

If that he say he cannot sing
Sum oder sport then let him bring
That it may please at this festing,
For now is the time of Christmas.

If he say he can nought do,
Then for my love aske him no mo,
But to the stockes then let him go,
For now is the time of Christmas.

Anonymous, Sixteenth Century

Magi

Joseph was the Famous Grouse,
and the Virgin Mary, the Babycham deer.
Standing in for the sheep and the ass
were the Black & White distillery terriers.

The shepherd loitering shyly with a lamp
was McEwan's Laughing Cavalier
and the followed star was a golden Harp,
the swaddling cloth, a Smithwick's towel.

Up on the walls where they hung all year
were Pio, Pearse and Johnny Walker
carrying whiskey, liberty and prayer;
gifts befitting an Irish saviour.

Colette Bryce

Happy Carp Christmas

Prague

Usually you buy it
a couple of days
before Christmas
and throw it in the bath.
The children
give it a name
something like Marek the carp
and spend hours in the bathroom
falling head over heels
in love with it.
Then father kills it.

No one wants
to eat it,
especially the children.
It tastes of shit:
we call it the bottom eater.
No presents till
you've eaten your carp!

Everybody's shouting.
It's full of tiny bones
which get stuck
in the throat,
some people choke to death.

Happy Carp Christmas
to everyone!
Happy Crap Christmas
to everyone!

Julian Stannard

Christmas Pudding

Stand in compressions of winter
like that woman in the shadow who keeps the light
alight
at this dark time in the North;
mix song and fairytale,
and blood, blood's taste,
the iron residual in dried fruit,
planets of glacé cherries,
pegs of suet;
throw the flat moon with the dead king's head
to the pudding's lump deep.
Stout is in, Hesperides' incurable dark;
Gawain's smell of boozy breath,
the knights in the dead wood (in essence)
at his lord's high table.

Sean Borodale

A Chair in Snow

 A chair in snow
should be
like any other object whited
& rounded

and yet a chair in snow is always sad

more than a bed
more than a hat or house
a chair is shaped for just one thing

to hold
a soul its quick and few bendable
hours

perhaps a king

not to hold snow
not to hold flowers

Jane Hirschfield

The Ghost Song

"The singers and workers that never handled the air"
                              - Gwendolyn Brooks

From a dream of summer, of absinthe,
I woke to winter. Carol singers
decked the walls of some long lost homeland,
late night shoppers and drowsy workers
headed for the train.
                    So the night that
you died was two faced, June light never
far from mind though snow fell. I handled
grief like molten sunshine, learned to breathe
your high lithe ghost song from thinnest air.

Paula Meehan

The Lineage

Child, stardust, small wonder
you look up tonight
to wish on old light.
I sense your grandmother's spirit
in the room. Time
has made her into prayer for us.

A wish and a prayer at Christmas
and you, too, either or both.
I hoped for nothing more.

The ancient law:
the mass cannot be sung
without the wax
because the lineage of bees
is from Paradise.

Carol Ann Duffy